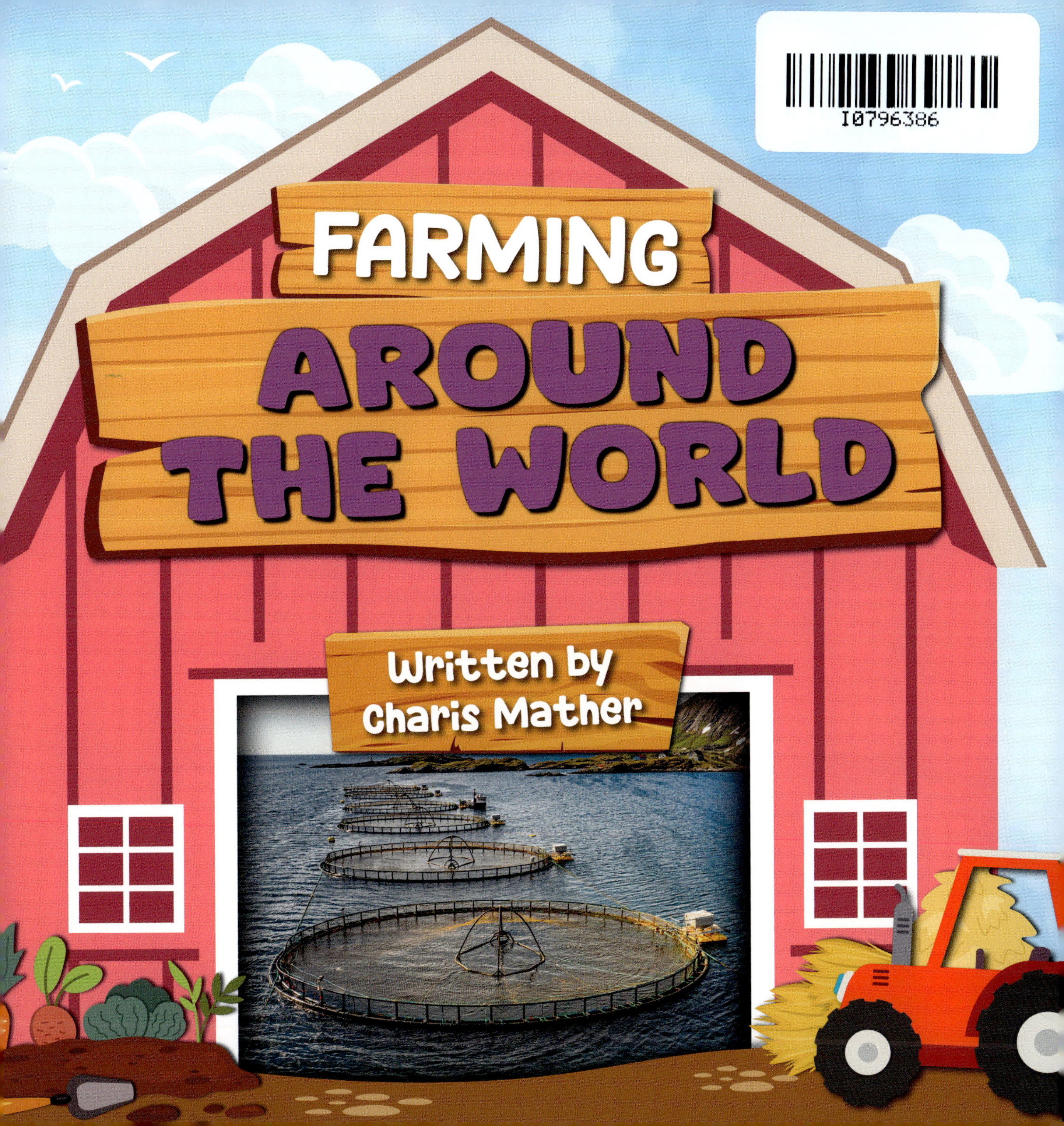
I0796386
FARMING
AROUND THE WORLD
Written by
Charis Mather

Library of Congress Control Number:
The Library of Congress Control Number is available on the Library of Congress website.

ISBN
979-8-89359-422-5 (library bound)
979-8-89359-442-3 (paperback)
979-8-89359-481-2 (epub)
979-8-89359-462-1 (hosted ebook)

Printed in the United States of America
Mankato, MN
012026

sales@northstareditions.com
888-417-0195

Written by:
Charis Mather

Edited by:
Noah Leatherland

Designed by:
Ker Ker Lee

Image Credits – Images courtesy of Shutterstock.com, unless otherwise stated.

Cover & Recurring – Ysami, Belozer, PCPartStudio, yusufdemirci, Tatiana Vizir, Alyona, Anatolir, Hybrid_Graphics, Andrei Armiagov, Sabelskaya, Antonov Maxim. 4–5 – Kikujiarm, Vadim Petrakov. 6–7 – Aleksandr Rybalko, Thampitakkull Jakkree, Andrei Armiagov, Sk Hasan Ali, Emily. 8–9 – Marie Wilson, Abie Davies, longtaildog. 10–11 – Viacheslav Lopatin, isoon kawsuk, Arif_Vector, Byrka Ekaterina. 12–13 – Mazur Travel, Daniel Prudek, JurateBuiviene, Evgeniy_D, Alaydruus. 14–15 – Dudarev Mikhail, Gigra, AerialVision_it, Yuriy Kulik. 16–17 – 1000 Words, Pierre Jean Durieu, SasinTipchai. 18–19 – Mariusz Bugno, WhiteYura. 20–21 – Jelena Stanojkovic, Kristi Blokhin, Perfect_kebab. 22–23 – Tomas Vynikal, Angel DiBilio.

CONTENTS

Words that look like <u>this</u> can be found in the glossary on page 24.

FARMING IS FASCINATING

There are many kinds of farms around the world. Some farmers make enough for just themselves. Others sell their goods. They might sell goods locally. Some farmers sell around the globe.

Wherever they are and however they farm, farmers need to know a lot. They must know all about the land, animals, and equipment they work with. Let's learn about this fascinating job.

AGRICULTURE AROUND THE WORLD

Agriculture includes both land and animal farming. The climate determines what kind of plants and animals can grow and live in an area.

Some farmers work on flat land. Others farm on hills. Some farmlands can be watery. Others can be hot and dry.

Some goods are common, such as corn and rice. Other goods can grow only in certain places. This is because of the different environments around the world.

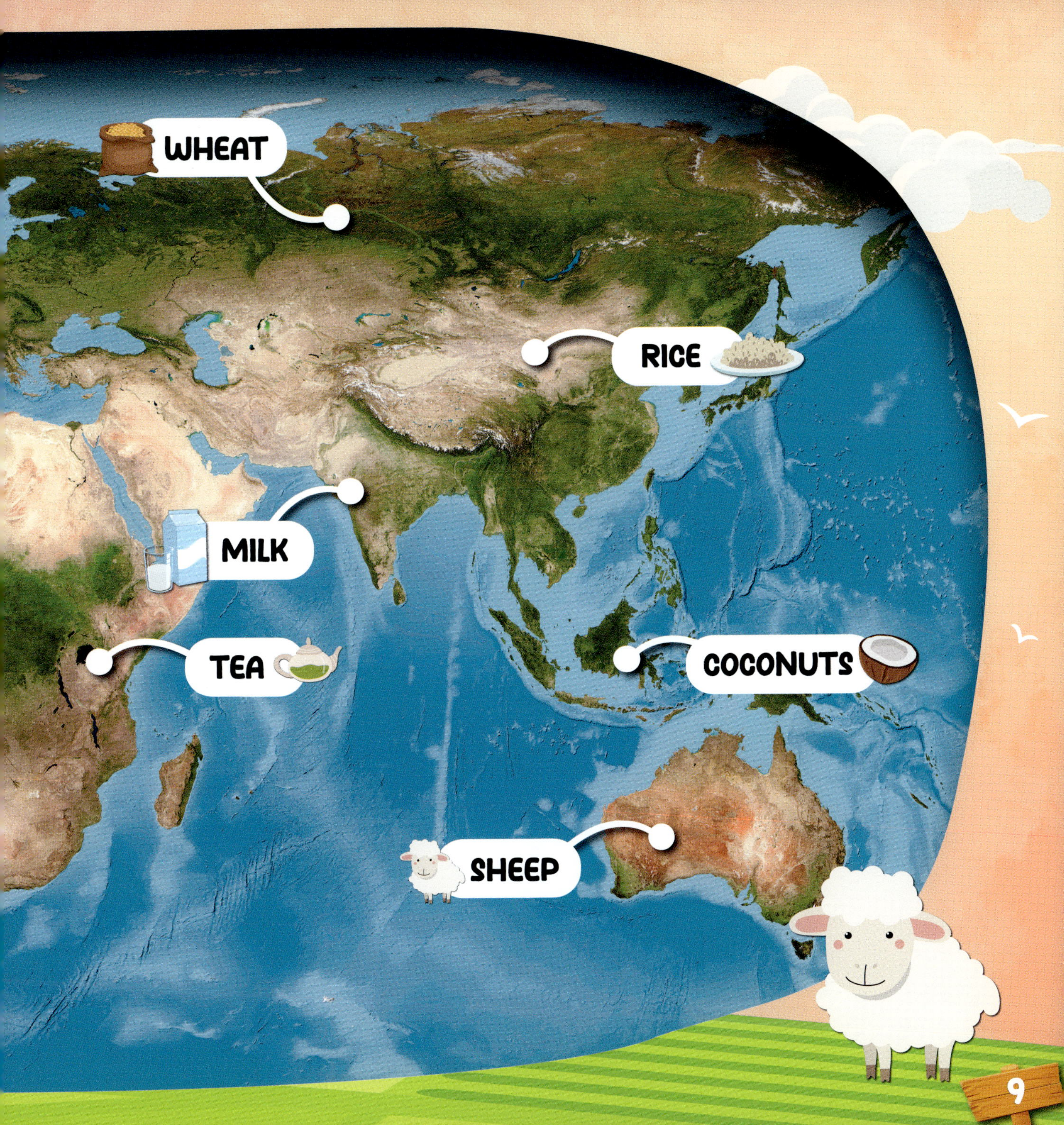
WHEAT
RICE
MILK
TEA
COCONUTS
SHEEP

DIFFERENT CLIMATES

Different crops may need different kinds of climates.

Tropical fruits need warm and wet environments. Mangoes and bananas are tropical fruits.

Some crops can be farmed in hot, dry climates, such as cacti and dates.

Winter crops grow well in cold weather. Cabbage is one example.

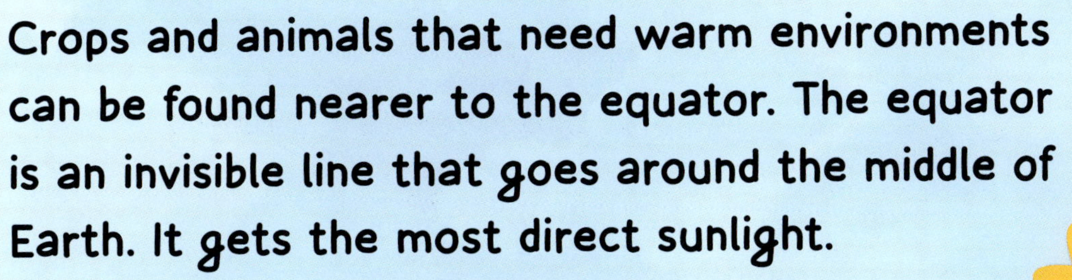

Crops and animals that need warm environments can be found nearer to the equator. The equator is an invisible line that goes around the middle of Earth. It gets the most direct sunlight.

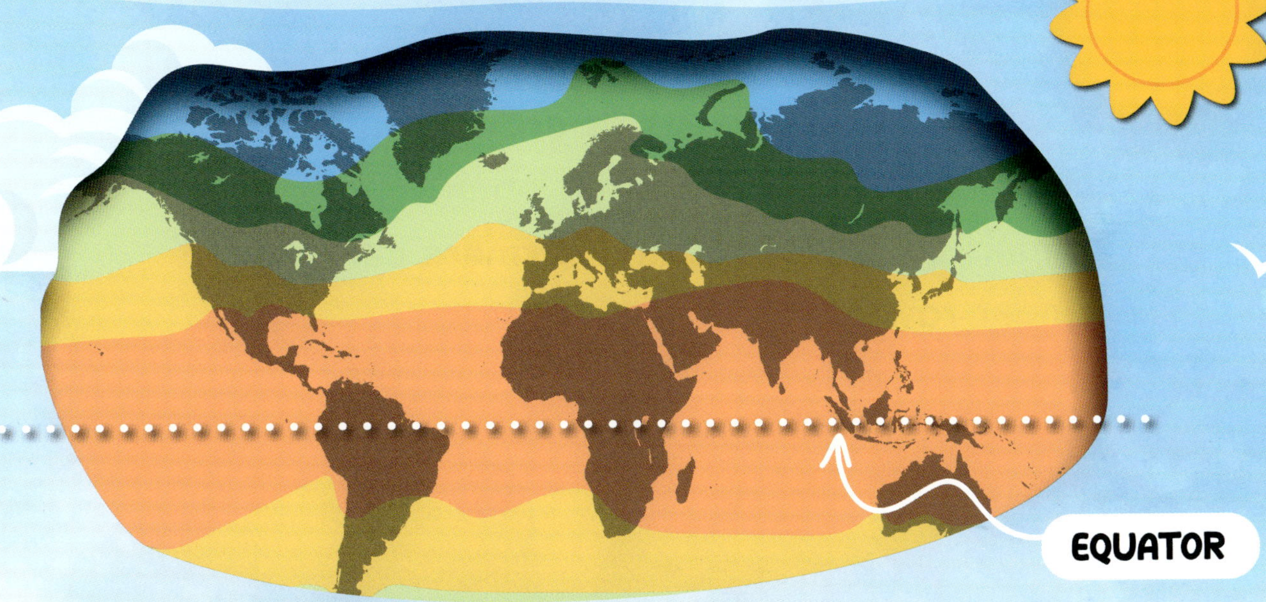

Camels live in deserts. Some camels are farmed for milk.

DIFFERENT LANDSCAPES

Farmers usually farm animals or grow grains and vegetables on flat land. The large open spaces allow animals to wander easily. Farmers can grow crops in neat rows.

In hilly places, farmers might turn land into terraces. Terraces are large steps on mountainsides.

Many terrace farms grow rice or grapes.

Hills are more difficult to grow crops on than flat land. So, farmers sometimes use hills to farm livestock.

DIFFERENT PRACTICES

Different kinds of farming practices are used around the world. Practices differ based on the environment, culture, and equipment in an area.

Nomadic Farming

Nomadic farming involves constantly traveling to find enough food for livestock.

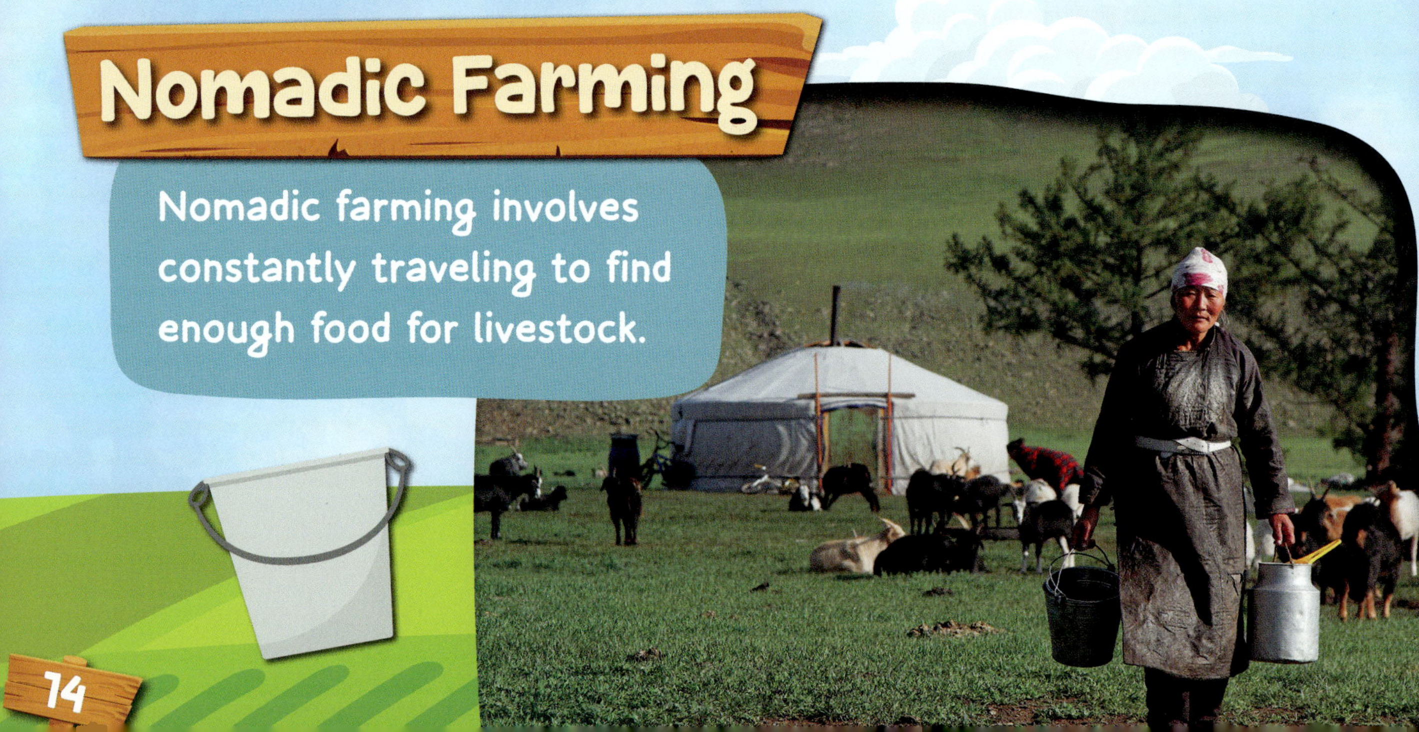

Mechanized Farming

Mechanized farming makes farming easier and faster by the use of machines. Machines can break up soil and plant seeds. They can spray water and gather crops.

Manual Farming

Manual farming uses human or animal workers and simple tools.

GLOBAL GOODS

Not every country can farm all the goods they want. So, countries buy goods from other places around the world. This is called importing. Selling goods outside a country is called exporting.

Most of Egypt is desert. It can be hard to grow crops there. So, Egypt imports a lot of food.

Importing also allows countries to get seasonal foods all year long. When it is winter in one part of the world, it is summer in another part. So, countries sell each other seasonal foods.

Strawberries often grow best in summer, but they are traded year-round.

SELLING LOCALLY

Some farmers prefer to sell locally. They don't have to send their goods far. The goods are usually very fresh. Farmers' markets are great places to find locally farmed food.

Buying locally is also a way for communities to help small farms. Goods from big farms are often cheap and easy to get. It can be hard for small farms to make money.

DEALING WITH DIFFICULTIES

Farmers face many difficulties, such as bad weather, disease, and pests. In some places, disasters such as floods and fires may ruin farms.

Pests are insects and other animals that destroy plants.

Farmers who sell goods around the globe make sure the goods are well-packaged for long journeys. If their goods go bad while they are being transported, farmers won't make money.

Agricultural goods are often transported in refrigerated boxes on ships and trucks.

WORKING HARD AROUND THE WORLD

Farming practices and the challenges that come with them are not the same everywhere. Some farmers worry about not growing enough crops. Others may have trouble transporting their goods safely.

Whatever the challenges, farmers all around the world have the same goal. They all work hard to make their farm a success.

GLOSSARY

climate the common weather in a certain place

communities groups of people who live and work in the same places

crops plants that are grown on a large scale to be eaten or used

culture the traditions, ideas, and ways of life of a group of people

environments the different parts of the natural world

goods products, often to sell

grains small fruits or seeds of some plants, such as wheat and rice

livestock animals that are kept for farming

locally near the area where someone lives

INDEX